PIGS

BY GAIL GIBBONS

HOLIDAY HOUSE   NEW YORK

FOR LARRY CHASAN

Special thanks to Daniel J. Kelly, D.V.M. of
Stonecliff Animal Clinic, Bradford, Vermont and
Joan, Ben and Larry Whiting's pigs of
West Topsham, Vermont.

Copyright © 1999 by Gail Gibbons
ALL RIGHTS RESERVED
Printed in the United States of America
Library of Congress Cataloging-in-Publication Data
Gibbons, Gail.
Pigs / by Gail Gibbons. — 1st ed.
p.   cm.
Summary: Examines the basic characteristics, common breeds,
intelligence, behavior, life cycle, and uses of pigs.
ISBN 0-8234-1441-8 (reinforced)
1. Swine—Juvenile literature. [1. Pigs.] I. Title.
SF395.5.G53   1999   98-28807   CIP   AC
636.4—dc21
ISBN 0-8234-1554-6 (pbk.)

ISBN-13: 978-0-8234-1441-3 (hardcover)
ISBN-13: 978-0-8234-1554-0 (paperback)

A PIG is also called a HOG or a SWINE.

Many people think pigs are smelly and dirty. They think pigs "eat like pigs" and aren't very smart. That's because they don't know pigs!

WILD BOAR

A TUSK is a very long tooth used for digging and fighting.

The wild boar is the animal from which all domestic pigs descended.

It is believed people started taming, or domesticating, pigs about 8,000 years ago. Often they were raised for food. People made things out of their hides, too.

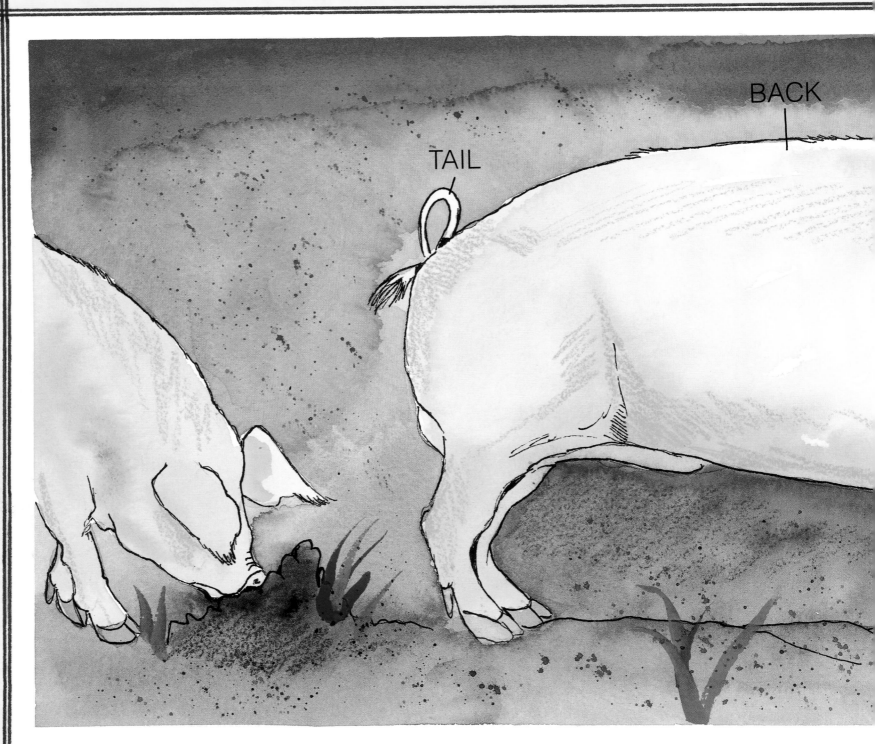

There are about 300 different breeds of pigs, but all pigs have the same basic characteristics. They have a heavy, round, bristly-skinned body with a round, flat nose called a snout. Pigs can use their snouts to dig up, or root, food out of the ground.

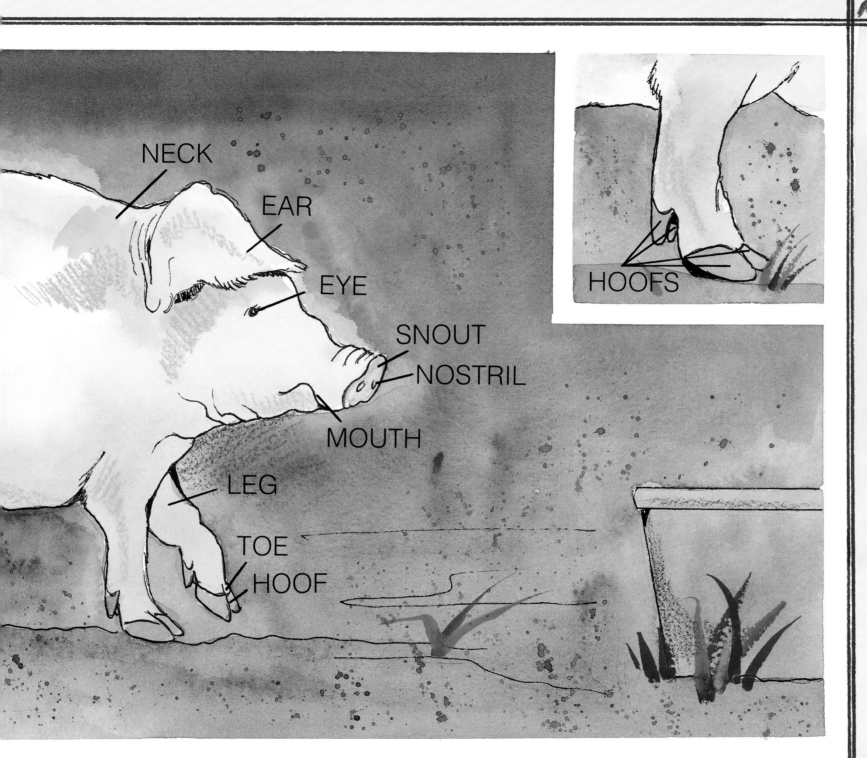

NECK

EAR

EYE

SNOUT

NOSTRIL

HOOFS

MOUTH

LEG

TOE

HOOF

Pigs have four toes on each foot. There is a hard hoof at the end of each toe. Only the two long middle hoofs are used for walking. And, of course, many pigs have wiggly, curly tails.

Before a female has babies, called piglets, she is called a gilt. After she has babies she is called a sow. Some sows can weigh up to 400 pounds or 180 kilograms (180 kg).

Male pigs are called boars. Some can weigh 900 pounds (405 kg) or more.

SOME COMMON BREEDS OF PIGS

LANDRACE PIG

GLOUCESTER OLD SPOT PIG

DUROC PIG

BERKSHIRE PIG

Pigs differ in size and color.

A BREED is a group of animals that share many traits.

TAMWORTH PIG

HAMPSHIRE PIG

CHESTER WHITE PIG

POLAND CHINA PIG

Each breed has some special characteristics.

Pigs are the smartest of all farm animals. Some scientists believe they are smarter than dogs. They can be taught to do many tricks.

Some pigs come when they are called. Others follow their owners around just like dogs. They can even be taught to roll over, retrieve, and pull a cart.

Pigs are tidy creatures and would much rather be clean all the time. Pigs should be given a clean place to live, with a pond or tub of water available.

When it gets too hot, pigs need to moisten their skin or they will get sick. They need to roll around in water to lower their body temperature. This is called wallowing. If there is no fresh water available, they will become desperate and wallow in sloppy, wet mud.

Oink! Pigs make sounds to communicate. They make grunting sounds to show pleasure or give a warning. Sometimes they make woeful cries when they're unhappy. When they are distressed, they make shrill squeals.

Pigs have good hearing. They have small eyes and poor eyesight. Some pigs have beautiful, long eyelashes.

Pigs have a very good sense of smell. A pig's snout is made up of tough cartilage covered with tiny sensitive pores. The snout is used as a scenting organ and a digging tool. In France some people use pigs to locate and dig up an unusual food called truffles.

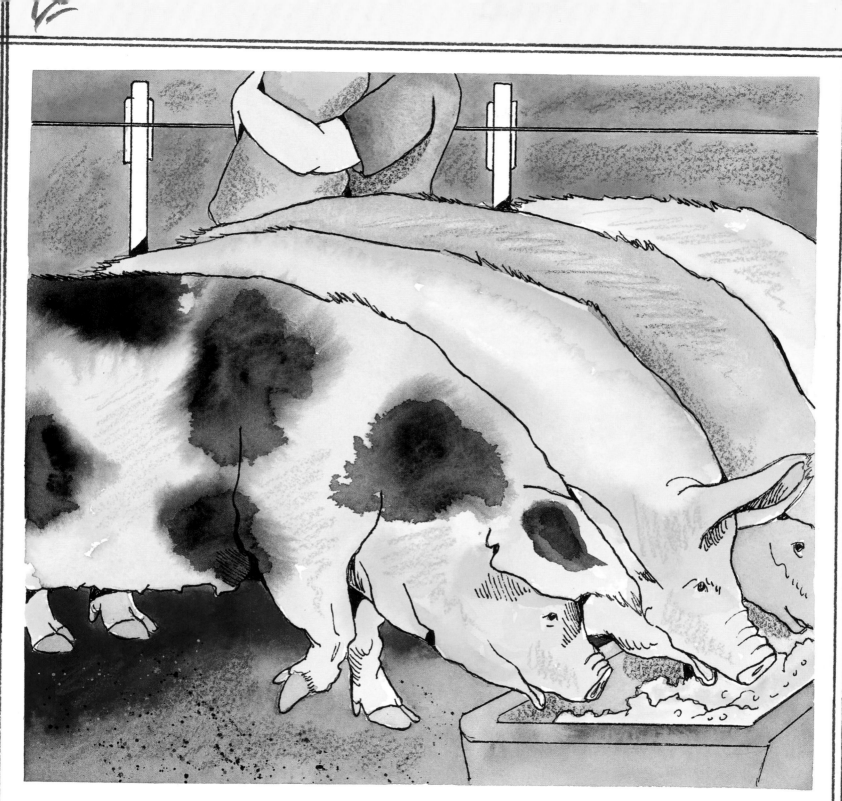

Farmers feed their pigs corn, cereal grains and soybean meal. Pigs love table scraps, too. Pigs don't "eat like pigs." They only eat as much as they need.

STY also called
PIGPEN

When there are only a few pigs, farmers keep them in sties, also called pigpens.

ARK

When there are lots of pigs, they are kept outside in a field that has little huts called arks. Sometimes they are kept in huge air-conditioned buildings.

A boar and gilt must be at least six months old to mate. The female farrows, or gives birth, to a litter of six to fifteen piglets. Each weighs about three and one-half pounds (1.5 kg).

PIGLET

At this time each piglet's two tiny and sharp "needle teeth," also called "wolf teeth," are cut so the piglets won't injure each other or their mother. Right away they begin drinking their mother's milk. For the first three weeks, the piglets completely depend on their mother for food. When they begin to stop nursing, they are weaning.

The piglets begin to copy the way their mother eats. They may root with their tender, tiny pink snouts foraging for food. They also begin to eat the food the owners bring.

Pigs grow more quickly than any other kind of farm animal. When the piglets are about six weeks old, they are weaned and weigh about 35 pounds (15.7 kg), ten times more than they weighed at birth. By the time they are six months old, they will be really heavy, about 200 pounds (99 kg).

SHOULDER

FAT BACK

LOIN

HAM

BACON

SPARERIBS

Most pigs are raised to go to market to become food for people to eat. Their hides may be used to make things such as gloves.

Some pigs never go to market. They may be kept as family pets or for showing.

What fun it is to go to a country fair! Often there are livestock shows. Pigs are cleaned and groomed to be judged.

The best pigs win ribbons or other awards. They are beautiful pigs.

It's fun to watch piglets romp about. They are cute and lovable with their curly tails, their flat pink snouts and their noisy squeals and grunts.

Soon they will grow to be big, big pigs.

OINK . . . OINK . . . OINK . . .

The ancient Egyptians used pigs to help them plant crops. Their little hoofs made holes just the right size and depth for seeds.

Pigs were brought to the New World in 1493 by Christopher Columbus on his second voyage. Later, many more were imported from England.

In the wild, pigs travel in herds of five to twenty. The males protect the females and their piglets.

Wild pigs can be found in most parts of the world. Some wild pigs are the wild boar, the warthog, the forest hog, the river hog and the babirusa. All of them can be very dangerous.

There is a children's story called *The Three Little Pigs*.

There are about 800 million domestic pigs in the world.

The record weight for a pig is about 2000 pounds (900 kg).

A pig can run as fast as 30 miles per hour or 48 kilometers (48 km). It is a good swimmer too.

A pig can live over 15 years.